30 Days with a Great Spiritual Teacher

Abide in

D1072966

• • • • • • • • •

The Gospel Spirituality of

JOHN THE EVANGELIST

JOHN KIRVAN

ave maria press AMP **notre dame, indiana**

JOHN KIRVAN, who conceived this series and has authored most of its titles, writes primarily about classical spirituality. His other recent books include *God Hunger*, *Silent Hope*, *Raw Faith*, and *There Is a God, There Is No God*.

Unless otherwise indicated, the scripture texts have been freely developed from the earliest English translations.

© 2006 by Quest Associates

All rights reserved. No part of this book may be used or reproduced in any manner whatsoever, except in the case of reprints in the context of reviews, without written permission from Ave Maria Press ®, Inc., P.O. Box 428, Notre Dame, IN 46556.

Founded in 1865, Ave Maria Press is a ministry of the Indiana Province of Holy Cross.

www.avemariapress.com

ISBN-10 1-59471-098-8 ISBN-13 978-1-59471-098-8

Cover and text design by Katherine Robinson Coleman

Printed and bound in the United States of America.

Library of Congress Cataloguing-in-Publication Data

Kirvan, John J.
  Abide in love : the Gospel spirituality of John the Evangelist / John Kirvan.
    p. cm. — (Thirty days with a great spiritual teacher)
  ISBN-13: 978-1-59471-098-8 (pbk.)
  ISBN-10: 1-59471-098-8 (pbk.)
  1. Bible. N.T. John—Meditations. 2. Devotional calendars. I. Title. II. Series: 30 days with a great spiritual teacher.

  BS2615.54.K57 2006
  242'.5—dc22

2006008494

Contents

*Let us not
love in word nor in speech,
but in deed
and in truth.
Let us live in truth,
even when our hearts
try to persuade us otherwise.
Let us live in truth knowing that
God is greater than our hearts
and knows all things.*

JOHN THE EVANGELIST

John the Evangelist

It might be more satisfying if we knew for certain that the apostle we call John the Evangelist was the author of the works that we love and continue to study for their spiritual wisdom.

However, the fact that we don't know who actually wrote these soul-shaping documents becomes irrelevant. It may be frustrating, but it is not crucial to our spiritual journey.

What we do know is far more important than what we don't know.

We know that all through the works which we attribute to John, there is a singular, distinctive, and passionate vision of what it is like to love and be loved by God.

It is a vision that warrants our calling him the Beloved Apostle. In Da Vinci's classic Last Supper it is John who rests his head on the shoulders of Jesus. We envy him. We want to join him at the table. We want to be caught in God's embrace.

In this simple image, John tells us something about God that we desperately want to hear. God is approachable. God loves us.

It is a theme that runs through every page of John's gospel. It is a theme that is meant to color every page of our lives, especially our prayers.

For some, the spiritual wisdom of John will best be encountered in a systematic reading of all of his works. No words will be left unstudied. But for others, those for whom this book has been especially prepared, John's words will be a source of spiritual inspiration and encouragement.

Here are thirty meditations chosen from the words of John, not in some specific order, but selected for their capacity to stimulate our daily prayer.

You may want to choose your own sequence. You may want to shape your own meditations. Choose what appeals to you, what inspires you, what opens your heart to prayer, and what gives hope to your day.

Discover as John did that we need not be afraid in the presence of God.

God, the Word Made Flesh, is capable of friendship. In that comfort, our spirituality takes shape and strength.

We hear the Word, just as John heard the Word.

In the beginning was that Word, and the Word was with God, and the Word was God.

This above all was what John knew, what John taught.

What follows, therefore, is not an attempt to weave a theology from the pages of scripture. It is rather a series of meditations woven from the reflections of the apostle John and recorded in the sacred writings of his gospel and his epistles.

This is how he prayerfully remembered what it was like to spend his days with Jesus.

This is John's invitation to join him in prayer.

Let us pray.

How to Pray This Book

The purpose of this book is to open a rich resource for its readers and to make accessible to today's spiritual seeker the experience and wisdom of John the Evangelist as it was recorded in the fourth gospel and in the epistles he sent to his followers.

Specifically, it has been written to stimulate and support your prayer life by drawing upon John's life, wisdom, and words as rich resources of ideas and themes to be meditated upon, to be contemplated, and to become the scriptural support of your daily search.

This is, therefore, not a book for mere reading. It invites you to meditate and pray its words on a daily basis for a period of thirty days.

It is a handbook for a spiritual journey.

Before you read these spiritual guidelines, remember that this book is meant to free your spirit, not to confine it. If on any day the meditation does not resonate well for you, turn elsewhere to find a passage that seems to better fit the spirit of your day and your soul. Don't hesitate to repeat a day as often as you like until you feel that you have discovered what the Spirit, through the words of the evangelist, has to say to your spirit.

Here are suggestions for one way to use this book as a cornerstone of your prayers.

As Your Day Begins

As the day begins, set aside a quiet moment in a quiet place to read the meditation suggested for the day.

The passage is short. It never runs more than a few hundred words, but it has been carefully selected to give a spiritual focus—a spiritual center to your whole day. It is designed to remind you, as another day begins, of your existence at a spiritual level. It is meant to put you in the presence of the spiritual master who is your companion and teacher on this journey. But most of all, the purpose of the passage is to give the words a chance. After all, you are not just reading this passage, you are praying it. You are establishing a mood of serenity for your whole day. What's the rush?

All Through Your Day

Immediately following the day's reading, you will find a single sentence which we have chosen to call a mantra, a word borrowed from the Hindu tradition but now in wide use in the West. This phrase is meant as a companion for your spirit as you move through a busy day. Write it down on a 3" x 5" card or on the appropriate page of your daybook. Look at it as often as you can. Repeat it quietly to yourself and go on your way.

It is not meant to stop you in your tracks or to distract you from responsibilities, but simply and gently to remind you of the presence of God and your desire to respond to this presence.

As Your Day Is Ending

This is a time for letting go of the day.

Find a quiet place and quiet your spirit. Breath deeply. Inhale, exhale—slowly and deliberately, again and again, until you feel your body let go of its tension.

Now read the evening prayer slowly, phrase by phrase. You will recognize at once that we have woven into it phrases taken from the meditation with which you began your day and the mantra that has accompanied you all through your day. In this way, a simple evening prayer gathers together the spiritual character of the day that is now ending as it began—in the presence of God.

It is a time for summary and closure.

Invite God to embrace you with love and to protect you through the night.

Sleep well.

Some Other Ways to Use This Book

1. Use it any way your spirit suggests. As mentioned earlier, skip a passage that doesn't resonate for you on a given day, or repeat for a second day, or even several days, a passage whose richness speaks to you. The truths of a spiritual life are not absorbed in a day or, for that matter, in a lifetime. So take your time. Be patient with the Lord. Be patient with yourself.

2. Take two passages and/or their mantras—the more contrasting the better—and "bang" them together. Spend time discovering how their similarities or differences illumine your path.

3. Start a spiritual journal to record and deepen your experience of this thirty-day journey. Using either the mantra or another phrase from the reading that appeals to you, write a spiritual account of your day, or a spiritual reflection. Create your own meditation.

4. Join millions who are seeking to deepen their spiritual life by joining with others to form a small group. More and more people are doing just this to support each other in their mutual quest. Meet once a week, or at least every other week, to discuss and pray about one of the meditations. There are many books and guides available to help you make such a group effective.

Thirty Days with
John the Evangelist

Day One

My Day Begins

Dear friends . . . the Word has been made flesh.

In the beginning was the Word.
The Word was with God,
and the Word was God.

He was with God in the beginning.
Through him all things came to be,
not one thing had its being
but through him.

All that came to be had life in him,
and that life was the light of all people,
a light that shines in the darkness,
that darkness could not overpower.

A man came sent by God.
His name was John.
He came as a witness,
as a witness to speak for the light
so that everyone might believe through him.
He was not the light,
only a witness to speak for the light.

The Word was the true light
that enlightens all people,
and he was coming into the world.

He was in the world
that had its being through him,
and the world did not know him.
He came to his own domain,
and his own people did not accept him.

But to all who did accept him,
who believed in his name,
he gave power to become children of God,
born not of human stock,
nor urge of the flesh,
nor of human will,
but of God himself.

—John 1:1–13

All Through the Day

His word is made flesh.

My Day Is Ending

Here in the gathering silence of this night,
let not my heart be troubled,
nor let it be afraid.

With your beloved John,
let me be caught up in your love.

I know I need not look for you.
You are waiting for me
in the silent dark.

You have been here
from the beginning.
You have been here
at every moment of this day.

Not one thing has had its being
except through you.
All that has come to be
has taken its life from you,
a life that is the light of all,
a light that shines in the dark,
that darkness cannot overpower.

Your word is the true light
That enlightens all of us.

Your word is the light
that cannot be overcome by the dark.
Hear my prayer.

Day Two

My Day Begins

Dear friends, . . . God is light.

I write to you about the Word of life,
which has existed from the very beginning.
We have heard it;
we have seen it with our eyes;
yes, we have seen it
and our hands have touched it.

When this life became visible we saw it.
So we speak of it

and tell you about the eternal life
that was with the Father and
was made known to us.

What we have seen and heard
we announce to you also,
so that you will join with us
in the fellowship
that we have with the Father
and with his Son, Jesus Christ.

We write this in order
that our joy may be complete.

Now the message
that we have heard from his Son
and announce to you is this:

God is light,
and in God there is no darkness at all.
If we say that
we have fellowship with him,
yet at the same time live in darkness,
we are lying,
both in our words
and in our actions.
But if we live in the light,
just as he is in the light,
then we have fellowship with one another,
and the blood of Jesus, his Son,
purifies us from every sin.

—1 John 1:1–10

All Through the Day

There is no darkness in him.

My Day Is Ending

Here in the gathering silence of this night,
let not my heart be troubled,
nor let it be afraid.

With your beloved John,
let me be caught up in your love.

Let me understand
that you and you alone
are the light
that I have so long sought.

You are the light,
you are God.

There is no darkness in you.

Let me understand
that you are the word
that I have so long sought to hear.

You are the Word Made Flesh.

I have seen you
and I have heard you.

It is time to speak
of what I have seen and heard.
It is time to speak of you.
Hear my prayer.

Day Three

―■―

My Day Begins

Dear friends, . . . I am the way, the truth, and the life.

"In my Father's house there are many mansions.
If not, I would have told you;
because I go to prepare a place for you.
And if I go and prepare a place for you,
I will come again
and will take you to myself;
that where I am you also may be.
And you know the way
where I am going."

Thomas said to him,
"Lord, we know not where you go,
so how can we know the way?"
Jesus said to him,
"I am the way, the truth, and the life.
No one comes to the Father but by me.

"If you had known me
you would, without doubt, have known the Father also.
And from now on you shall know him
for you have seen him."

Philip said to him,
"Lord, show us the Father
and that will be enough for us."
But Jesus said to him,
"Have I been with you so long

and you have not known me?
Philip, whoever sees me, sees the Father also.
How can you say: 'Show us the Father'?
Do you not believe
that I am in the Father
and the Father is in me?
The words that I speak to you,
I speak not of myself.
The Father, who abides in me, does the works.
Amen, amen, I say to you,
the works that I do you also will do
and greater than these."

—John 14:1–12

◆◆◆◆◆

All Through the Day

You are the way, the truth, and the life.

◆◆◆◆◆

My Day Is Ending

Here in the gathering silence of this night,
let not my heart be troubled,
nor let it be afraid.

I need not go on looking
for a way to live.
You are the way.

I need no longer search
for the truths that I have pursued
all the days of my life.
You are the truth.

I need not
live in fear of death.
You are life.

But there is something I must do.
I must let go of fear—
and without reservation.
I must stop searching
for what I have already found.

Only in you can I find
the way, the truth, and the life.

You alone can show me our Father.
Hear my prayer.

Day Four

My Day Begins

Dear friends, . . . I give you a new commandment.

"Now is the son of man glorified," he said,
"and God is glorified
in him."

If God is glorified in him,
God also will glorify him in himself
and will immediately glorify him.

"A new commandment I give you,
that you love one another.

"By this all people will know
that you are my disciples,
if you have love one for another.

"Little children, yet a little while
I am with you.
You shall seek me;
and as I said to the Jews
so I say to you now,
where I go you cannot come."

Simon Peter said to him,
"Lord, where are you going?"
Jesus answered,

"Where I am going
you cannot follow now,
but you will follow later."

Peter said to him,
"Why cannot I follow you now?
I will lay down my life for you."

Jesus answered him,
"Would you lay down
your life for me?
Amen, I say to you:
the cock will not crow
before you deny me three times."

—John 13:31–38

All Through the Day

Have love, one for another.

My Day Is Ending

Here in the gathering silence of this night,
let not my heart be troubled,
nor let it be afraid.

With your beloved John,
let me learn the meaning
of your new commandment:
love one another.

By this all will know
that we are your disciples—
if we love each other.

But there is another side to the story.
I am an undependable lover.

Like Peter, I am as ready to deny you
as to praise you.
For all my promises and good intentions,
before the end of this night,
like Peter, chances are I will have denied you.

Mine is a story of two hearts,
a classic tale of a willing heart and a fragile heart.
In my humanity
they seem always to go together.
My promises go hand in hand with my denials.
But here in the silent darkness,
let me try. Again.
Hear my prayer.

Day Five

My Day Begins

Dear friends, . . . what I now write down for you is nothing new.

It is an old commandment,
one that you have heard from the beginning:
Love one another.

Darkness has passed,
and the true light now shines.
So now anyone who claims to live in the light
and hates another is still in the dark.

Anyone who loves another
lives in the light,
and there is nothing in that one
that would hurt another.

However, anyone who hates another
lives in the dark
and walks aimlessly in the dark,
blinded by the darkness.

I write to you, the little children,
because your sins are forgiven.
I write to you, the fathers,
who have known him from the beginning.
And I say to the young people
who have overcome the wicked ones:
Love not the world

nor the things of this world,
for the love of God cannot live
in anyone who loves the world.

All that is in the world
is the lust of the flesh and of the eyes,
the pride in riches.

None of this is of the Father, but of the world.
The world and its lusts will pass away,
but the one who does the will of God
will live forever.

—1 John 2:7–17

All Through the Day

Darkness has passed.

My Day Is Ending

Here in the gathering silence of this night,
let not my heart be troubled,
nor let it be afraid.

Let me fall asleep tonight
knowing that I have nothing to be afraid of,
knowing that darkness has passed
and the true light now shines.

Let me fall asleep tonight
knowing that the world
that I have so often trusted,
that I have so often surrendered to,
has lost its power over me.

You have promised
that if I do the will of God,
if I do your will,
if I love my brother or sister,
if there is nothing in my life
that would hurt another,
I will live forever.

There is nothing new in this promise.
But here in the darkness of this night
I need to hear again
that there is nothing to be afraid of.

The true light now shines.
Hear my prayer.

Day Six

My Day Begins

Dear friends, . . . I have chosen you.

This is my commandment:
Love one another
as I have loved you.

Greater love than this
no one has,
to lay down one's life
for one's friends.

You are my friends
if you do the things that I command you.
I will not call you servants,
for a servant does not know
what the master does.
But I have called you friends
because everything I have heard from my Father
I have made known to you.

You have not chosen me.
I have chosen you
and appointed you to go forward
and bring forth good fruit.
And your fruit should remain.

Whatever you may ask of the Father
in my name he will give to you.

This I command you,
that you love one another.
If the world hates you,
know that it hated me before you.
If you had been of the world,
the world would have recognized you as its own.
But I have chosen you out of the world.
Because you are not of the world
the world hates you.

Remember what I have said to you.

—John 15:12–20

All Through the Day

You have called me friend.

My Day Is Ending

Here in the gathering silence of this night,
let not my heart be troubled
nor let it be afraid.

Rather, let me take heart
from your unimaginable promise of friendship.

Here in the night
I wonder how this can be.
Who am I
that you should call me friend?
What do you see in me
that I cannot see?

Why have you chosen me?
What is it that you want of me?

What do you expect of a friend?

I am puzzled
and a little afraid of the dark.
But this I know:
You are here
in the silent darkness of this night.
You are here as a friend.

I need not be afraid to surrender
to the mystery of your love
and to your promise of friendship.
Hear my prayer.

Day Seven

My Day Begins

Dear friends, . . . love is of God.

If we are to love God,
we must first love one another,
for love is of God.
Anyone, therefore, who loves,
is born of God and knows God.

But he who does not know love
does not know God.

God our Father knows us
and loves us.

No one of us has ever seen him,
but he has sent
his only begotten Son into the world
so that we might live by him,
loving one another and repenting of our sins.

God loves us.
Not because we have first loved him.
Rather, he has first loved us.

We have seen and testify
that the Father has sent his only begotten Son
to be the savior of the world,
to show us how to love one another
as God loves us.

And if any of us says, "I love God,"
but does not love another,
that one is a liar.
For how can we love God,
whom we cannot see,
if we cannot love our brothers and sisters
whom we can see?

This is the commandment
that we have from God:
"Love one another."

—1 John 4: 7–12, 20–21

All Through the Day

He has first loved me.

My Day Is Ending

Here in the gathering silence of this night,
let not my heart be troubled
nor let it be afraid.

I have nothing to fear.
I am not alone.
No one is.

You have sent your Son
to be with us,
and by loving us,
to teach us what love is.

You have taught us
that to love you
is to love one another.

To love you
is to be a child of God,
to know God.

Teach me to love
as you have loved.

For whoever does not love
does not know God,
does not know you.
Hear my prayer.

Day Eight

My Day Begins

Dear friends, . . . we need not remain in darkness.

Many of the authorities
who heard Jesus believed him,
but because of the Pharisees
they did not confess their faith in him
to avoid being cast out of the synagogue.

For they loved the glory of the world
more than the glory of God.

As Isaiah predicted,
their eyes were blinded
and their hearts hardened.
They did not see with their eyes
or understand with their hearts.

Jesus, who alone could heal them,
cried out: "Whoever believes in me,
believes not in me but in him who sent me.

"I have come as light into the world
so that whoever believes in me
may not remain in darkness.

"I do not judge any man who hears my words
and keeps them not,
for I came not to judge the world
but to save the world.

"Whoever despises me
and does not receive my words
is already judged by the word I have spoken.
The same words shall judge that one on the last day.
I have not spoken of myself,
but of the Father who sent me.
He commanded what I should say
and what I should speak.

"I speak as the Father has spoken to me."

—John 12:42–50

All Through the Day

Open my eyes.

My Day Is Ending

Here in the gathering silence of this night,
let not my heart be troubled
nor let it be afraid.

With your beloved John,
let me be caught up in your love.

Here in the darkness of the night
I am aware of my blindness
and the hardness of my heart.

Centuries ago Isaiah warned us
it would be like this.
Our eyes, he said,
would be blinded,
our hearts hardened.

We will not see with open eyes
or understand with an open heart.

But here in the dark silence of this night
there is something that has not changed.
You are still present in every corner of my life;
if I choose, I have your eyes to see with.

I still have your heart to hope and love with;
I still have your words to pray with.
Hear my prayer.

Day Nine

My Day Begins

Dear friends, . . . whoever hears my word has life everlasting.

The Father loves the Son
and shows him everything that he himself does,
and greater works than these
will he show him,
so that you may wonder.

For as the Father raises up the dead
and gives life,
so the Son also gives life to whom he wills.

For the Father does not judge anyone,
but has given all judgment to the Son,
that all may honor the Son
as they honor the Father.

Whoever honors not the Son
honors not the Father who has sent him.
Amen, amen, I say to you:
Whoever hears my word,
and believes in the one who sent me,
has life everlasting and will not be judged,
but rather passed from death to life.

Amen, amen, I say to you:
The hour is coming and is already here
when the dead shall hear
the voice of the Son of God.

They who hear shall live,
for as the Father has life in himself,
so too has he granted to the Son
to have life in himself.

Wonder not at this;
for the hour is coming
when all who are in the graves
shall hear the voice of the Son of God.

They who have done good things
will come forth to the resurrection of life;
and they who have done evil will be judged.

—John 5:20–29

All Through the Day

. . . that we may wonder.

My Day Is Ending

Here in the gathering silence of this night,
let not my heart be troubled
nor let it be afraid.

With your beloved John,
let me be caught up in your love.

With him
let me be caught up in the everlasting life
that you have promised
to all who will listen to
and hear your words.

This night, with all its silence,
is all about life.
It is all about being raised from the dead,

all about being raised from the death
that I so eagerly cling to.

The hour has come
and is already here
when the dead
shall hear the voice of the Son of God.

When I hear your voice,
I shall come alive
in the silence of this night.
Hear my prayer.

Day Ten

My Day Begins

Dear friends, . . . whoever believes in me has eternal life.

Your ancestors ate manna in the desert
and they are dead.
This bread comes down from heaven.
Whoever eats this bread
will not die.

I am the living bread
that has come down from heaven.

Anyone who eats this bread
will live forever,
for the bread that I will give
is my flesh
for the life of the world.

Amen, amen, I say to you:
Unless you eat the flesh of the Son of Man
and drink his blood,
you shall not have life in you.

If you eat my flesh
and drink my blood
you have everlasting life,
and I will raise you up on the last day.

For my flesh is food indeed,
and my blood is drink indeed.
Those who eat my flesh
and drink my blood
abide in me
and I in them.

—John 6:47–56

All Through the Day

Anyone who eats this bread
will live forever.

My Day Is Ending

Here in the gathering silence of this night,
let not my heart be troubled
nor let it be afraid.

With your beloved John,
let me be caught up in your love.

Slowly, very slowly
I am learning that
only the love that you bring to the table
can feed the hunger of my soul.

I can no longer
settle for anything less.
I am no longer content

to get up from the table unnourished,
my hunger for you unsatisfied.

The manna that fed the desert people
is not enough.

Only the food that you have promised,
that you alone can offer,
only your own body and blood
is enough to satisfy the hunger
you have stirred in my soul.
You are the bread of my life.
Hear my prayer.

Day Eleven

My Day Begins

Dear friends, . . . ask whatsoever you desire.

I am the true vine,
and my Father is the vinedresser.

Every branch in me
that does not bear fruit he will cut away,
and every branch that does bear fruit
he will trim, that it may bring forth more fruit.

Now you are clean by reason of the word
I have spoken to you.

Abide in me
and I in you.
As the branch cannot bear fruit of itself
unless it abides on the vine,
so neither can you unless you abide in me.

I am the vine;
you are the branches.
If you abide in me
and I in you
you will bear much fruit.
For without me you can do nothing

If you do not abide in me,
you will be cut off and will wither.
They will gather you up

and cast you into the fire.
And you will burn there.

But if you abide in me
and my words abide in you
you will ask for whatever you desire
and it will be done.

In this is my Father glorified:
that you bring forth much fruit
and become my disciples.
As the Father has loved me,
I also have loved you.
Abide in my love.

—John 15:1–9

All Through the Day

Abide in my love.

My Day Is Ending

Here in the gathering silence of this night,
let not my heart be troubled
nor let it be afraid.

Rather, let me take heart
from your promise of unending love
and your gift of peace.
Let me be unafraid to surrender
my soul to the mystery of your love
and your promise of peace.

I want to be with you,
but I know it is not something I can earn,
not a reward for being good.

You are the vine.
I am just a branch
that cannot grow
apart from your love.

As the branch cannot bear fruit of itself
unless it abides in the vine,
so neither can I
unless you abide in me,
and I in you.

This is not an easy truth for me to embrace.
I want to earn your love,
but I must accept it as a gift.
Hear my prayer.

Day Twelve

![square]

My Day Begins

Dear friends, . . . we are of God.

Because there are many false prophets
at work in the world,
it is important
not to believe every spirit,
but rather to test the spirits
to see if they are of God.

Only those who profess
that Jesus Christ is God come in the flesh
are to be believed.

Every spirit that denies
that Jesus is of God
is of the Antichrist.
You have heard that he is coming;
he is already here.

Those who are of the world
speak to the world,
and the world hears them.

But you, my children,
who are of God,
have overcome the Antichrist

because Christ who is in you
is greater than the one
who is in the world.

We are of God,
and those who know God
will hear us.
Those who are not of God
will not hear us.

You must test the spirit
to discover who is
and who is not of God,
who will hear you
and who will not.

—1 John 4:1–6

All Through the Day

I am your child.

My Day Is Ending

Here in the gathering silence of this night,
let not my heart be troubled
nor let it be afraid.

There is nothing to be afraid of.
I am your child.

Your power and your love
are at work within me.
They need only my choosing
to set them loose
wherever I go,
whatever I do.

Whether I am of you
or of the world
is my choice.

I can be of you,
or not.
Here in the silence of this night
I can say:
I am of God,
I am of Christ,
I am of you.

If I choose.

Hear my prayer.

Day Thirteen

My Day Begins

Dear friends, . . . we must be born anew.

Now there was a ruler of the Pharisees
named Nicodemus who came to Jesus by night
and said to him: "Rabbi, we know
that you are a teacher come from God;
for no one can do the signs that you do
unless God is with him."

Jesus answered him: "Truly, truly, I say to you:
No one can enter the kingdom of God
without being born from above."

Nicodemus said to him:
"How can anyone be born who has grown old?
Can one enter a second time into the mother's womb
and be born again?"

Jesus answered:
"Unless one is born of water and the Holy Spirit,
one cannot enter the kingdom of God.

"What is born of the flesh is flesh,
and what is born of the spirit is spirit.
Do not marvel that I said to you:
You must be born anew.

The wind blows where it will
and you hear the sound of it,
but you do not know where it comes from,
or where it goes.
So it is with everyone who is born of the spirit.

"I say to you:
we speak of what we know
and bear witness to what we have seen.
But you do not receive our testimony.

"If I have told you earthly things
and you do not believe,
how can you believe
if I tell you heavenly things?"

—John 3:1–12

All Through the Day

The wind blows where it will.

My Day Is Ending

Here in the gathering silence of this night,
let not my heart be troubled
nor let it be afraid.

Rather, let me take heart
from your promise of unending love
and your gift of peace.

Let me be unafraid to surrender
my soul to the mystery of your love
and your promise of peace.

But I know it will not be easy.
You are asking me
to change my mind,
to change my heart,

to turn my life,
my whole way of seeing,
upside-down.

You are telling me that
I must begin
to see my life and my world
as you see them.

I must be born again.

Hear my prayer.

ABIDE IN LOVE

Day Fourteen

My Day Begins

Dear friends, . . . anyone who is born of God will be kept by God.

I write these things to you
so that you who believe
in the name of the Son of God
may know that you have eternal life.

This is how confident we are in him:
We know that he will hear
whatever we ask
that is according to his will.

We know that if we see
our brother sinning, but not to death,
God will give him life.

We know that there is a sin to death,
that the whole world
is in the powers of evil,
but that anyone
who is born of God
will be kept by God,
and the evil one
will not touch him.

We know that the Son of God
has come
and has enabled us

to understand him
who is true.

We are in him
who is true.

We are in his Son, Jesus Christ.

He is the true God.
His is eternal life.

—1 John 5:13–20

All Through the Day

Hold me.

ABIDE IN LOVE

My Day Is Ending

Here in the gathering silence of this night,
let my heart not be troubled
nor let it be afraid.

I know that after the darkness
I will awaken to a new day.

But I have no illusions.
It will be the same old world.

I am born into and live my life
in a world ruled by idols,
by false Gods,
by substitutes for you.

But I accept no substitutes.
I am your child.
You are the true God.
You, only you,
have eternal life.
That is what I seek.

In the darkest of nights
there is something I can rely on.
I know that anyone who is born of you
will be kept by you.

Hold me in your hands.
Hear my prayer.

Day Fifteen

My Day Begins

Dear friends, . . . faith overcomes the world.

In this we know
that we love the children of God:
when we love God
and keep his commandments.

For this is the love of God,
that we keep his commandments.
And his commandments
are not a heavy burden.

For whatever is born of God
overcomes the world.
And this is the victory
that overcomes the world—our faith.

Who is the one who overcomes the world?
It is the one who believes
that Jesus is the Son of God.

Jesus Christ
came not by water only,
but by water and blood
and by the Spirit also.
The Spirit testifies that
Christ is the truth.

There are three
that give testimony:
the Spirit,
the water,
and the blood.
These three agree.

We accept human testimony,
but the testimony of God is greater.

—1 John 5:2–10

All Through the Day

Christ is the truth.

My Day Is Ending

Here in the gathering silence of this night,
let not my heart be troubled
nor let it be afraid.

Above all,
let me not surrender to the world
I bring with me.

It will be hard.
I know that I enter this night
weighed down by the world
and its promises,
weighted down by a day,
by a life of little surrenders.

Only you
can break the stranglehold
that the world has on my soul.

Free me.
I am your child.
I believe in you.
Lift the burden
of my surrenders to the world.

Grant me the victory
which overcomes the world—
faith in you.

Hear my prayer.

Day Sixteen

My Day Begins

Dear friends, . . . follow what is good.

From God the Father
and from Christ Jesus,
the Son of the Father,
in truth and in charity,
and for the sake of the truth
that dwells in all of us
and that will remain with us always,
may grace, mercy, and peace be with you.

We have been commanded
to walk in the truth,
to love one another.
This is not a new commandment.

It is the one that
we have heard from the beginning.

But beware,
there are many seducers in the world
who do not follow this commandment,
who do not love one another,
who do not confess with you
that Jesus Christ
has come in the flesh.

My dearly beloved,
follow not what is evil
but what is good.
Whoever does good is of God.
Whoever does evil does not see God.

Peace be with you.
Above all do not lose sight of
the commandment that you have known
all your years.

Let us love one another.

—2 John 3-6

All Through the Day

Walk in the truth.

My Day Is Ending

Here in the gathering silence of this night,
let not my heart be troubled,
nor let it be afraid.

Here in the silence your voice is clear:
We are to love one another,
but I hardly hear you.
Maybe it is because I have heard
this commandment since my childhood
and have grown used to it.
It has become commonplace.

Perhaps it is because
in some small corner of my heart
I hear your commandment

and whisper to myself that it is impossible.
It is too much to ask.

Or maybe it is too little.
Perhaps when I hear it spoken
in the dark silence of this night
I think: This can't be all there is,
there must be something more.
And your voice cuts through the darkness.

"There's nothing more.
This is all there is.
But it is enough."

Hear my prayer.

Day Seventeen

My Day Begins

Dear friends, . . . lift up your eyes.

There came a time
when Jesus gathered his disciples together
and said to them:
"I have food to eat,
which you do not know about.
My food is to do the work
of him who sent me.
My food is to perfect that work.

"You who say there are yet four months to go
before it will be harvest time,
I tell you:
Lift up your eyes
and see that the fields
are already ripe for the harvest.

"You will reap a harvest
That you did not sow
and gather its fruit
to life everlasting.

"Both the one who sows
and the one who reaps
will rejoice together.

For in this the saying is true:
One sows, another reaps.
I have sent you
to reap a harvest
you did not labor over.
Others have labored
and you have entered
into the fruits of their labors.

"This is the will
of him who sent me."

—John 4:32–37

All Through the Day

I will reap what he has sown.

My Day Is Ending

Here in the gathering silence of this night,
let not my heart be troubled
nor let it be afraid.

But most of all,
in the quiet dark of this night,
remind me that I am not alone,
that I am completely dependent on you,
that without you I am nothing.

Without you I can do nothing.

It is not an easy admission.

It is not an easy surrender.

I am destined to reap a harvest
that I have not sown.

It is your harvest.

In this the saying is true:
One sows, another reaps.

Hear my prayer.

Day Eighteen

My Day Begins

Dear friends, . . . go on your way.

On one occasion at Capernaum
there was a certain ruler whose son was sick.
Having heard that Jesus
had come from Judea into Galilee,
he sought him out
and begged him to come down
and heal his son,
for he was at the point of death.

Jesus said to him:
"Unless you see signs and wonders,
you do not believe."

The ruler asked again:
"Lord, come down before my son dies."

Jesus said to him:
"Go on your way, your son lives."

The man believed what Jesus said to him
and went on his way.
And as he went on his way
his servants brought him word
that his son lived.
He asked them therefore:
"At what hour did my son grow better?"

124

They answered: "The fever left him yesterday
at the seventh hour."

The father realized that it was at that same hour
that Jesus had said to him: "Your son lives."

The ruler believed,
and with him his whole household.

—John 4:46–53

All Through the Day

Not in signs and wonders. . . .

My Day Is Ending

Here in the gathering silence of this night,
let not my heart be troubled,
nor let it be afraid.

Let me be confident of your presence,
confident that I will be able to find you
in the silence of this night.

I don't want to be one of those
who have to see signs and wonders
before I believe that you are here,
that you care,
that you can be reached
here in the night.

I need to find you
in the ordinariness of the day just past
and of this night.

I need to find you
where you are,
not where I expect you to be,
not in signs and wonders,
but in the silent darkness
of this night.

Hear my prayer.

Day Nineteen

My Day Begins

Dear friends, . . . do for others as I have done for you.

Before the festival day of Passover,
Jesus, knowing that his hour had come
when he would pass out of this world to the Father,
having loved his disciples,
he loved them to the end.

"You call me master and Lord," he said to them,
"And you do well, for so I am.

"But amen, amen, I say to you:
The servant is not greater than his lord,
nor is the apostle
greater than the one who sent him."

Knowing that the Father
had given all things into his hands,
and that he came from God
and would return to God,
he rose from the supper table,
laid aside his garments,
took a towel and girded himself.
After that he put water into a basin
and began to wash the feet of his disciples
and to wipe them with the towel
with which he had girded himself.

In time he came to Simon Peter,
who said to him:
"You shall never wash my feet."

Jesus answered him:
"If I do not wash you,
you shall have no part with me."

Simon Peter said to him:
"Lord, not only my feet
but also my hands
and my head."

—John 13:1–9

All Through the Day

In time I will understand.

ABIDE IN LOVE

My Day Is Ending

Here in the gathering silence of this night,
let not my heart be troubled
nor let it be afraid.

With your beloved John,
let me be caught up in your love.

There is nothing very complicated
about what you do.
Rather, the spiritual path that you urge on those
who would follow you
is something very simple.

You don't tell us to write a theology text.
You say very simply:
"I have given you an example

that as I have done to you
so you should do for each other.
I have washed your feet.
Go, wash the feet of one another."

Do what I do.
That's the message you lived,
the message that I find so difficult to follow.
That's it.

Hear my prayer.

Day Twenty

My Day Begins

Dear friends, . . . you have heard what I said to you.

Those who love me
will keep my word,
and my Father will love them.
We will come to them
and make our abode with them.

Those who do not love me
do not keep my word.

The word that you have heard
is not mine,
but is the Father's who sent me.
These things I have spoken to you
while abiding with you.
But the Paraclete,
the Holy Spirit,
whom the Father will send in my name,
will teach you all things
and bring to mind all the things
that I have said to you.

Peace I leave you.
My peace I give you.
Not as the world gives do I give to you.
Let not your heart be troubled,

nor let it be afraid.
If you love me you will indeed be glad
because I go to the Father,
for the Father is greater than I.
Now I have told you before it comes to pass
that when it comes to pass you may believe.
I will not speak of many things to you now
for the prince of this world is coming.
He has no power over me,
but I do as the Father has commanded me
so the world may know
that I love the Father.

Arise, let us go hence.

—John 14:23–31

All Through the Day

My peace I give you.

ABIDE IN LOVE

My Day Is Ending

Here in the gathering silence of this night,
let not my heart be troubled
nor let it be afraid.

Instead, let me take heart
from your promise of unending love.
Let me be unafraid to surrender
my soul to the mystery of your love
and your promise of peace.
But let me remember
that your peace is not a gift
to be treasured, protected, hidden away.

It is not a gift
of tranquility, serenity, and passivity,

a kind of spiritual trophy.
It is instead a gift
that is meant to be given away,
shared, acted upon,
a gift meant to give shape to our lives
and to our world.

Your gift of peace is a gift of courage,
a kind of peace that the world does not recognize,
that it seldom encourages
and even more rarely honors.

Let me not be afraid.

Hear my prayer.

ABIDE IN LOVE

Day Twenty-One

My Day Begins

Dear friends, . . . you will have no need
for any teacher but the Spirit.

Dearly beloved:
It is the last hour.
The Spirit has anointed you.
You have heard that the Antichrist is coming
and, indeed, that many Antichrists are already in our midst.
They are not of us.
If they had been of us
they would undoubtedly have stayed with us.

I write to you
as someone who knows the truth,
who knows that Jesus is the Christ,
who knows that whoever denies the Son
denies the Father also.
As for you, let that promise
that you have heard from the beginning
abide with you.

I write these things
so that you will not be seduced
by those who do not tell the truth.
As for you, let the Spirit
with which God has anointed you
abide in you.
You will have no need for any other teacher.

The Spirit,
who is truth,
who does not lie,
will teach you all things.
Little children, abide with the Spirit,
so that when Christ appears
you may have confidence in him
and not be confounded by his appearance.
You know that he is just.
Know also that everyone who lives in justice
is born of him.

—1 John 2:18–29

All Through the Day

The Spirit has anointed me.

My Day Is Ending

Here in the gathering silence of this night,
let not my heart be troubled
nor let it be afraid.

For it is in silence that you speak,
it is with silence that you will teach my heart
what it most needs to know.
It is in your silence that I will hear you.

But only if I learn how to listen to the night.
Do not let me miss this opportunity.
Don't let me clutter the night with my words.

Teach me instead how to see in the dark,
how to listen to your silence.

In the midst of all those who
would lay claim to my heart,
let me hear you.
Let me hear the Spirit.
You will teach me
what I need to know.

I have no need for any other.
For you are the truth;
you do not lie.

Hear my prayer.

Day Twenty-Two

My Day Begins

Dear friends, . . . do whatever he tells you to do.

There was a marriage in Cana of Galilee
and the mother of Jesus was there.
Jesus and his disciples were also invited.
When the wine failed the mother of Jesus said to him:
"They have no wine."
Jesus said to her:
"Woman, what is that to me or to you?
My time has not yet come."

His mother turned to the waiters and said:
"Do whatever he tells you to do."

Now the hosts had set out
six large stone vessels to be used to fulfill
the Jewish manner of purification.
Each vessel held two or three measures.

Jesus said to the waiters:
"Fill the water pots with water."
They filled them to the brim.
Then Jesus said to them: "Draw out now
and carry them to the chief steward."
And they carried them.

The chief steward tasted the water made wine
without knowing from where it came.

The waiters knew where it came from
because they had drawn the water.
After tasting the water made wine,
the chief steward called the bridegroom
and said to him: "Every man
first sets out the good wine,
and only after his guests have drunk well,
does he set out the wine that is not so good.
You have kept the good wine until now."

It was in Cana of Galilee
that Jesus did this first miracle, thus manifesting his glory.

—John 2:1–11

All Through the Day

"Do whatever he tells you to do."

My Day Is Ending

Here in the gathering silence of this night,
let not my heart be troubled,
nor let it be afraid.

But I am afraid.

In the dark silence of this night,
I admit that it is hard for me to follow instructions,
hard for me to do what you tell me to do.
Hard for me to obey a God I cannot see.
So I cover my bets.

Here at the beginning of my journey
I am afraid to let go,
afraid to entrust my soul into your keeping.
I go on acting as though I know better than you.

But tonight, in this silent darkness,
your mother gives me courage.
"Don't be afraid," she says.
"Do what he tells you to do.

"It's okay.
You can trust my son.
He sees wine where you see only water."

Open my eyes.
Roll back the darkness.

Hear my prayer.

Day Twenty-Three

My Day Begins

Dear friends, . . . the Lord is our shepherd.

The Son of God has come
so that we may have life
and have it to the full.

"I am," he said, "the good shepherd.
The good shepherd is one who
lays down his life for his sheep.

"The hired man, since he is not the shepherd
and the sheep do not belong to him,
abandons the sheep and runs away
as soon as he sees a wolf coming.
And then the wolf attacks
and scatters the sheep.
This is because he is only a hired man
and has no concern for the sheep.
I am the good shepherd.
I know my own
and my own know me
just as the Father knows me
and I know the Father.

"And I lay down my life for my sheep.
There are other sheep I have

that are not of this fold
and these I have to lead as well.
They, too, listen to my voice,
and there will be only one flock
and one shepherd.
The Father loves me
because I lay down my life
in order to take it up again.
No one takes it from me.
I lay it down of my own free will
so it is in my power to take it up again.
This is the command
I have been given by my Father."

—John 10:11–18

All Through the Day

You are the shepherd of my soul.

My Day Is Ending

Here in the gathering silence of this night,
let not my heart be troubled,
nor let it be afraid.

With your beloved John,
let me be caught up in your love.

You are the shepherd of my soul,
the shepherd of all my soul's hopes and desires.

Here in the deepening darkness,
let me not forget:
You are the one who
has laid down his life for his sheep,
who has laid down his life for me.

It is not that I have loved you.
It is that you have loved me
with a love that is unquestioning.

You have come
so that I might have life
and have it to the full.

Here in the silence
hear my prayer.

Day Twenty-Four

My Day Begins

Dear friends, . . . only the Lord can satisfy our hunger.

On one occasion when his followers who had eaten
of the loaves and fishes sought him out,
Jesus reminded them that they should not
labor for the food that perishes,
but to do the works of God.
"What must we do," they asked,
"if we are to do the works of God?"

Jesus answered: "This is the work of God
that you believe in him whom he has sent."
So they said to him:
"If we are to believe in you,
what sign will you give us
that we may see and believe?
Our fathers ate manna in the wilderness;
as it is written,
'He gave them bread from heaven to eat.'"

Jesus then said to them:
"Truly, truly, I say to you: It was not Moses
who gave you the bread from heaven.
It is my Father who gives you
the true bread from heaven.

For the bread of God is
the bread that comes down from heaven
and gives life to the world."
They said to him; "Lord give us this bread always."

Jesus said to them:
"I am the bread of life.
Whoever comes to me will not hunger,
and whoever believes in me will never thirst."

—John 6:25–36

All Through the Day

We need never go hungry.

ABIDE IN LOVE

My Day Is Ending

Here in the gathering silence of this night,
let not my heart be troubled
nor let it be afraid.

You have fed us with loaves and fishes,
but the bread of this world
is not enough.
I hunger for more.
I hunger for you.

You have said that
you are the bread of life.
You have promised that
if I come to you

I shall not hunger;
if I believe in you
I shall never thirst.

I turn to you now,
in the silent darkness of this night
to ask you to keep your promise.
My soul hungers for what only you can give.

Hear my prayer.

Day Twenty-Five

My Day Begins

Dear friends, . . . we shall not thirst.

On one occasion Jesus came to Samaria,
to a place near the field
that Jacob gave to his son Joseph.
Jacob's well was there.
And so Jesus, wearied as he was from his journey,
sat down beside the well.
It was about the sixth hour.

There came to him a Samaritan woman
to whom Jesus said, "Give me a drink."
The woman said to him,
"How is it that you, a Jew,
ask a drink of me, a woman of Samaria?"

Jesus answered her: "If you knew the gift of God,
and who it is that is saying to you,
'Give me a drink,'
you would have asked him
and he would have given you living water."

The woman said to him:
"Sir, you have nothing to draw with
and the well is deep.
Where will you get that living water?
Are you greater than our father Jacob,

who gave us the well and drank from it himself,
and his sons and his cattle?"

Jesus said to her:
"Everyone who drinks of this water will thirst again,
but whoever drinks of the water
that I shall give will never thirst.
The water that I shall give
will become a spring of water
welling up to eternal life."

The woman said to him,
"Sir, give me this water, that I may not thirst
nor come here to draw."

—John 4:7–16

♦♦♦♦

All Through the Day

Give me living water.

♦♦♦♦

ABIDE IN LOVE

My Day Is Ending

Here in the gathering silence of this night,
let not my heart be troubled,
nor let it be afraid.

With your beloved John,
let me be caught up in your love.

But, like the woman
who came to you at the well,
I do not recognize you in the dark.
You are not what I expected.

You are too ordinary.
You are an ordinary man, a stranger,
hot and tired,

thirsty from the road,
a stranger in need of water.

I do not recognize you.

It is not as though
you hide yourself from me.
It is not as though
you wear a mask that must be lifted
if I am to recognize you.
You hide nothing.
You are everywhere and everyone.
You are too available.

Hear my prayer.

Day Twenty-Six

‖

My Day Begins

Dear friends, . . . God is generous.

In this have we come to know
the generosity of God,
the Son has laid down his life for us.
In turn we ought to lay down our lives
for our sisters and brothers.
For how could we say
that the love of God abides in us if,
having the things of this world,

we see our sister or brother in need
and nonetheless close our hearts to him.

My little children,
let us not love in word nor in speech,
but in deed and in truth.

Let us live in truth
even when our hearts
try to persuade us otherwise.

Let us live in truth, knowing that
God is greater than our hearts and knows all things.

Dearly beloved, if we are living in truth,
obeying his commandments,
and doing those things

that are pleasing in his sight,
we can have confidence in God.
Whatever we shall ask of God we will receive.

And this is the commandment that
the Spirit has given us:
We should believe in the name of his Son
and love one another.

Keeping his commandment
we can be confident that
the Spirit will abide in us
and we in the Spirit.

—1 John 3:16–24

All Through the Day

God is generous.

My Day Is Ending

Here in the gathering silence of this night,
let not my heart be troubled,
nor let it be afraid.

Grant me, I pray,
a quiet and peaceful night.
In my search for peace of soul,
do not let me
close my eyes and ears
to my brothers and sisters
and to all who are in need.

How can I say
that I live in you and you live in me,

if I see my brothers and sisters in need
and nevertheless close my heart to them?

It would be to live a lie.
I could not sleep in peace.

Let me love
not in word nor in speech,
but in deed and in truth.

Let me live and love in truth,
even when my heart
tries to persuade me otherwise.

Hear my prayer.

Day Twenty-Seven

My Day Begins

Dear friends, . . . God has given us his only Son.

God so loved the world
that he gave his only Son
that whoever believes in him
shall not perish
but have eternal life.

For God sent his Son into the world,
not to condemn the world

but that the world
might be saved
through him.

Whoever believes in him
is not condemned.
Whoever does not believe
is condemned already
because he has not believed
in the name of the only Son of God.

And this is the judgment:
The light
has come into the world
and people have loved darkness
rather than light.

Those who do evil
hate the light
and do not come
to the light,
lest their deeds should be exposed.

But those who do what is true
come to the light
that it may be clearly seen
that their deeds
have been done
in God.

—John 3:16–21

All Through the Day

The light has come into the world.

My Day Is Ending

Here in the gathering silence of this night,
let not my heart be troubled,
nor let it be afraid.

With your beloved John,
let me be caught up in your love.

In your embrace
let me find the courage
to tell the truth to my soul.

You are the light of the world,
but I have loved the darkness
rather than the light.

Do not condemn me.
Lead me instead to what is true.

And this is the truth:
No matter how dark the night,
you are light and you are here.

No matter how dark the night,
your love cannot be extinguished.

No matter how dark the night,
you are the light of the world.
You remain the light of my life.

Hear my prayer.

Day Twenty-Eight

My Day Begins

Dear friends, . . . our sorrow shall be turned into joy.

If I do not go
the Paraclete will not come to you.
But if I do go
I will send him to you.
Amen, amen, I say to you:
You will lament and weep,
but the world will rejoice.

And though you are sorrowful,
your sorrow will be turned into joy.

A woman, when she is in labor, has sorrow
because her hour has come.
But when she has brought forth her child
she no longer remembers the anguish
because of her joy at the birth of her child.

So also you now have sorrow indeed.
But I will see you again
and your heart will rejoice,
and that joy no one will be able to take from you.

I have spoken to you in parables.
But the time is coming
when I will no longer speak to you in parables,
but plainly about the Father.

Abide in Love

On that day I will speak to the Father on your behalf.
He loves you
because you have loved me,
and have believed that
I came from God.

I am from the Father.

Behold: The hour is coming,
and is now here.
These things I have spoken to you
that in me you may have peace.

—John 16:7–33

All Through the Day

My heart will rejoice.

My Day Is Ending

Here in the gathering silence of this night,
let not my heart be troubled
nor let it be afraid.

Rather, let me take heart.

For you have promised
that if I believe in you
and in your Father,
the sorrows and difficulties of this night
will pass.
The dark will give way to light.
Our sorrows
will be turned into the joy
of a new day.

But for now we are in labor.
We know with what pain
a new life comes into being.
We are being born again.
Our hour has come.
and it is now here.

You have overcome the world.
The darkness of this night will end.
As you promised, our sorrow
will become joy.

Hear my prayer.

Day Twenty-Nine

My Day Begins

Dear friends, . . . the light is among us.

The hour has come
when the Son of Man
will be glorified.

Amen, amen, I say to you:
Unless the grain of wheat
falls to the ground and dies,
it remains alone.

But if it dies
it will bring forth much fruit.

Those who love their life
will lose it;
and those who hate their life in this world
will keep it to life eternal.

Now is my soul troubled.
And what shall I say?
"Father, save me from this hour."
But it is for this reason
that I have come into this world.

Father, glorify my name.
If I be lifted up from the earth,
I will draw all things to myself.

Yet a little while
the light is among you.
Walk while you have the light
that the darkness not overtake you.

Those who walk in darkness
do not know where they are going.
Therefore, walk while you have the light.

Believe in the light.

—John 12:23–25, 27–36

All Through the Day

Whoever clings to life shall lose it.

My Day Is Ending

Here in the gathering silence of this night,
let not my heart be troubled,
nor let it be afraid.

With your beloved John,
let me be caught up in your love.

Here in the darkness of the night,
teach me about light and life.

Teach me that
unless I die to all the things
that I have clung to in the name of life
I will never know the new life that I seek.

Teach me that
if I am to live,
I must embrace death.
I must learn and accept
that my life is like a grain of wheat.
If it does not die,
there can be no flowering.
There can be no fruit.

Unless I die to the world,
there is no life.

Hear my prayer.

Day Thirty

My Day Begins

Dear friends, . . . we have heard the word of life.

Early on the first day of the week
following the death of Jesus, when it was still dark,
Mary Magdalene went to the sepulchre
where Jesus had been buried and discovered
that the stone had been taken from his tomb.

She ran to Simon Peter
and to the other disciple whom Jesus loved.

Weeping, she told them: "They have taken away our Lord,
and we know not where they have laid him."
Not knowing, as yet, the scripture
that said he must rise again from the dead,
they ran to the tomb.
They saw the linen cloths
lying on the ground, and they believed.

The disciples returned to their homes,
but Mary stayed by the empty tomb.
Turning, she saw a young man
whom she did not at once recognize as Jesus.

"Tell my disciples," he said to her,
"that you have seen the Lord.
I will ascend to my Father,
to my God and to your God."

In the days to follow, Jesus did and said many things.
If they were all written down,
the world would not be big enough
to contain the books that would have to be written.

But these few words
that I have recorded are written
that you may believe
that Jesus is the Christ, the Son of God,
and that in believing,
you may have life in his name.

—John 20–21

All Through the Day

I have life in his name.

My Day Is Ending

Here in the gathering silence of this night,
let not my heart be troubled
nor let it be afraid.

With your beloved Mary,
with John,
let me learn again what it means
to be caught up in your love
while it is still dark,
where so often I cannot remember
where they have laid you,
where we should look,
where we shall find you.

Let me remember that
Jesus is risen,
that the tomb is empty,
that Jesus lives,
that it is in him that
I, too, live.

Remind me that
I have seen you,
that you are the Christ, the Son of God,
and that in believing,
I might have life in your name.

Hear my prayer.

One Final Word

This book is meant to be nothing more than a gateway to the spiritual wisdom of the evangelist John.

You may decide that the way of John as described and developed in these pages is not what your spirit requires at this moment. But there are many other teachers, and many other traditions. Somewhere there is the right teacher for you—for your own, very special, absolutely unique journey. You will find your teacher; you will discover your path. We would not be searching, as St. Augustine reminds us, if we had not already found. In the end, however, there is no substitute for reading the scriptures and especially for discovering and exploring the spiritual world of John the Evangelist.

One more thing should be said.

Spirituality is not meant to be self-absorption, a cocoon-ish relationship of God and Me. In the long run, if it is to have meaning, if it is to grow and not wither, it must be a wellspring of compassionate living. It must reach out to others as God has reached out to us.

We have to break down the walls of our souls and let in not just heaven but the whole world.

True spirituality reaches out to all the children of God. It does not end in our own consolation but in that all-embracing love of others that we call compassion.

You May Want to Read

To follow up your interest in the words of John the Evangelist, you may want to read, study, and/or pray with one of the following books.

There is no substitute for going to the source—the full text of the New Testament. There are hundreds of editions of the New

Testament. You may find that one of these fits your spiritual needs:

The most scholarly: *The Jerusalem Bible* (Doubleday)

Most widely used: *The Revised Standard Version* (various publishers)

The most literary: *The Holy Bible* translated by Ronald Knox (Templegate Publishers)

The most accessible: *The Good News Bible: The Bible in Today's English* (The American Bible Society)

There is no question that for the serious student, the best accessible writing on John and his works comes from Raymond Brown. Look for his work in good libraries, in bookstores, and on the Internet. Then reward your self with the best there is.